MARSHES & SWAMPS

New & Updated

BY GAIL GIBBONS

HOLIDAY HOUSE NEW YORK

Special thanks to Thomas W. Doyle, PhD, Deputy Center Director,
Wetland and Aquatic Research Center, United States Geological Survey.

Thanks also to Mike Owen of the
Fakahatchee Strand State Preserve, Copeland, Florida.

To the kids of the Everglades City School, Florida

The Library of Congress has cataloged the previous edition as follows:

Gibbons, Gail.
Marshes and swamps / by Gail Gibbons.
p. cm.
Summary: Defines marshes and swamps, discusses how conditions in them
may change, and examines the life found in and round them.
ISBN 0-8234-1347-0
1. Marshes—Juvenile literature. 2. Swamps—Juvenile literature.
[1. Marshes. 2. Swamps.]   I. Title.
GB621.G53   1998   97-17995 CIP   AC
551.41—dc21

ISBN: 978-0-8234-4925-5 (hardcover)
ISBN: 978-0-8234-1515-1 (paperback)

WETLAND

MUD is wet SOIL.

Marshes and swamps are wetlands. They are made up of soaked, wet ground or are covered with shallow water over a muddy bottom. Plants take root in the mud and grow their stems, leaves, and flowers above the water.

MARSH

A marsh is made up of many grassy plants and sometimes a few shrubs. There are no trees or woody plants.

SWAMP

Swamps have trees, bushes, and shrubs and flood often. Most swamps begin as marshes when dead plants begin to pile up and decay or flooded trees die. As the area becomes shallower, trees, bushes, and shrubs can take root in the soil. They can grow to cover much of the marshy area, turning it into a swamp.

TUNDRA

DESERT MARSH

Wetlands are found throughout the world. Some of today's wetlands have existed for about 10,000 years. In the tundra of the far north, marshes form when frozen ground thaws and melts. Sometimes desert marshes form near a spring of water.

Marshes and swamps are found in open, wide lowlands, along seacoasts, and in the shallow edges of ponds, lakes, and rivers.

Marshes and swamps have different types of water. Some have fresh water, and some have salt water. Saltwater marshes form when ocean water mixes with fresh water from rivers.

FRESHWATER MARSHES

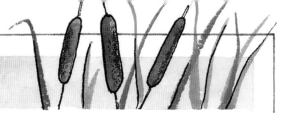

Freshwater marshes form around the shallow edges of lakes, rivers, and ponds. Some are no wider than a few feet. Others are huge . . . as far as you can see! The Everglades, in Florida, is the largest freshwater marsh in the United States. It is about 4,000 square miles.

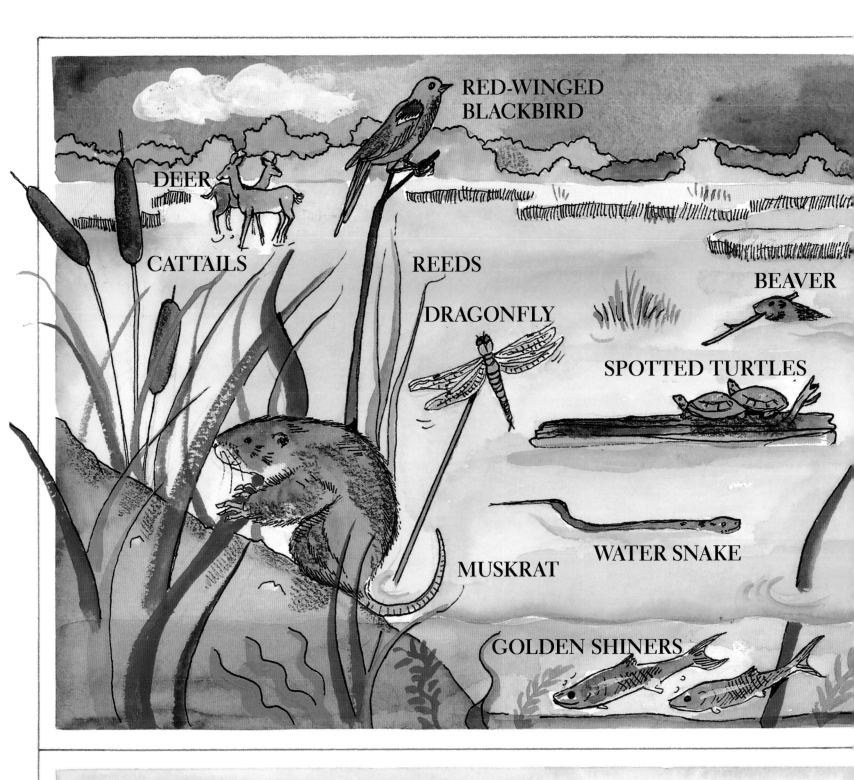

RED-WINGED BLACKBIRD

DEER

CATTAILS

REEDS

DRAGONFLY

BEAVER

SPOTTED TURTLES

WATER SNAKE

MUSKRAT

GOLDEN SHINERS

A freshwater marsh is made up of grassy plants such as reeds, cattails, duckweeds, and rushes. It is an ideal place for insects to live.

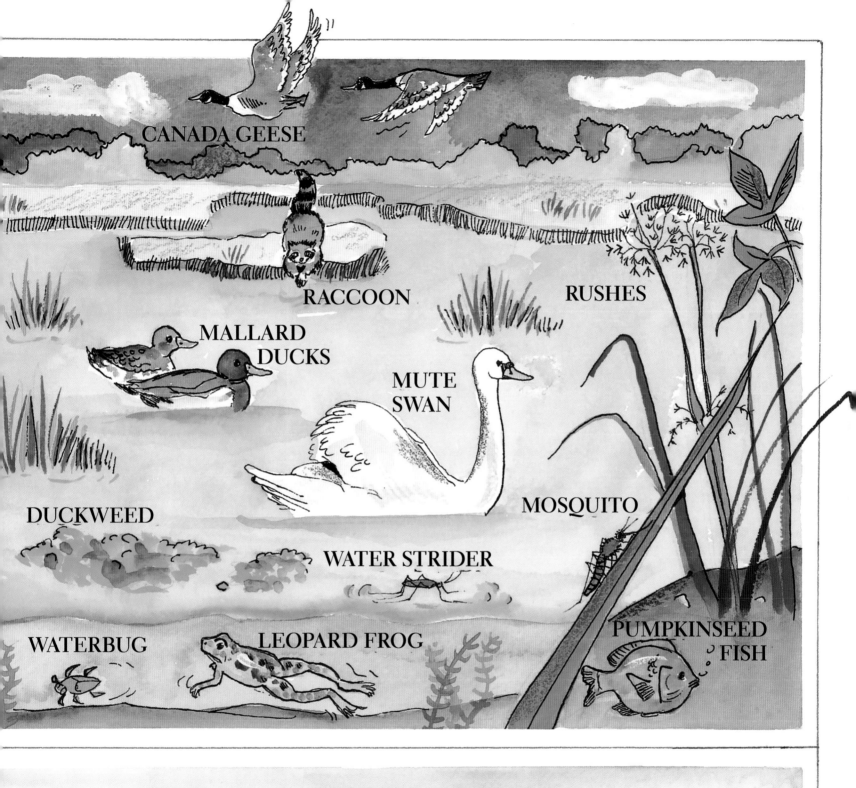

CANADA GEESE

RACCOON

RUSHES

MALLARD
DUCKS

MUTE
SWAN

DUCKWEED

MOSQUITO

WATER STRIDER

WATERBUG

LEOPARD FROG

PUMPKINSEED
FISH

Many different kinds of fish, birds, and other animals live, nest, and thrive in this environment.

SALTWATER MARSHES

HIGH TIDE

AMERICAN AVOCET

GULLS

LOW TIDE

Saltwater marshes are found along the coast. Tides cause water levels to rise and fall daily. At high tide a large part of the saltwater marsh is under water. During low tide much of the land is visible.

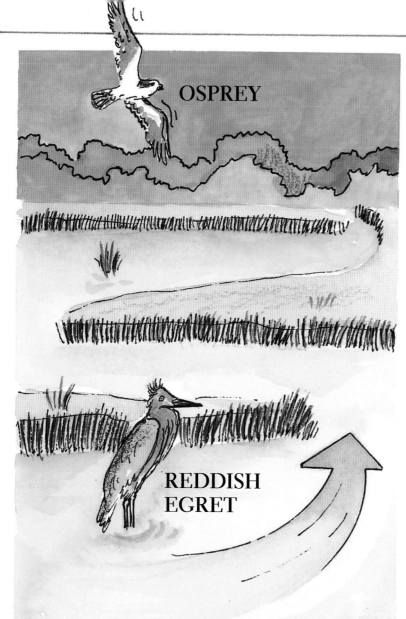

OSPREY

REDDISH
EGRET

SANDPIPERS

When the tide rises and enters a marsh, it brings salt water in, creating a rich, growing environment for the plants and creatures living there. When the tide reverses and the salt water drains back out to sea, it carries bits of dead plants and animals that become food for the fish that live in the ocean.

RING-BILLED GULL

OSPREY

BROWN PELICAN

OPOSSUM

SNOWY EGRET

FLOUNDER

MOSQUITO FISH

In the United States saltwater marshes are found along the East Coast, the Gulf of Mexico, the San Francisco Bay, the Pacific Northwest, and Alaska. That's because there is a lot of flat, low land near the shores. Saltwater marshes teem with all kinds of birds and marine life.

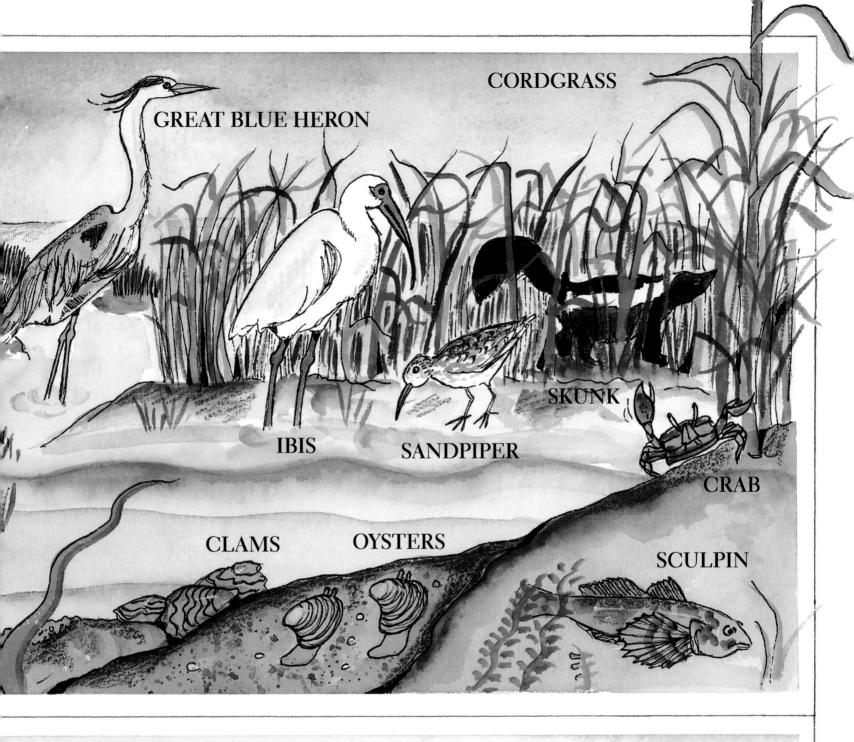

GREAT BLUE HERON

CORDGRASS

IBIS

SANDPIPER

SKUNK

CRAB

CLAMS

OYSTERS

SCULPIN

The plants, fish, and animals that live there have adapted to the daily rising and falling of the water.

FRESHWATER SWAMPS

Freshwater swamps are usually waterlogged. The water levels change with the amount of rainfall or river water they receive. Most trees and other plants will live as long as their roots aren't under water for long periods of time.

Different kinds of plants and animals are found in different swamps. In cooler swamps one might find silver maple, willow, and ash trees growing. Often, moose come to feed on swamp plants. There is a lot of wildlife.

RED MAPLE

BOBCAT

An EPIPHYTE is also called an AIR PLANT.

PANTHER

WOOD STORK

BALD CYPRESS TREE

WATER HYACINTH

COTTONMOUTH SNAKE

EGRET

SNAPPING TURTLE

DUCKWEED

LONGNOSE GAR

In some warm climates the bald cypress tree grows. Its special roots have stumpy shapes, called cypress knees, that stick up out of the water.

BARRED OWL

SPANISH MOSS

OTTERS

ALLIGATOR

CYPRESS KNEE

BULLFROG

CRAYFISH

Swamps are often dark and damp. All kinds of sounds are heard. A barred owl screeches. An alligator slaps the water. A bullfrog croaks. Birds peck at the mud and water for their food.

MANGROVE SWAMPS

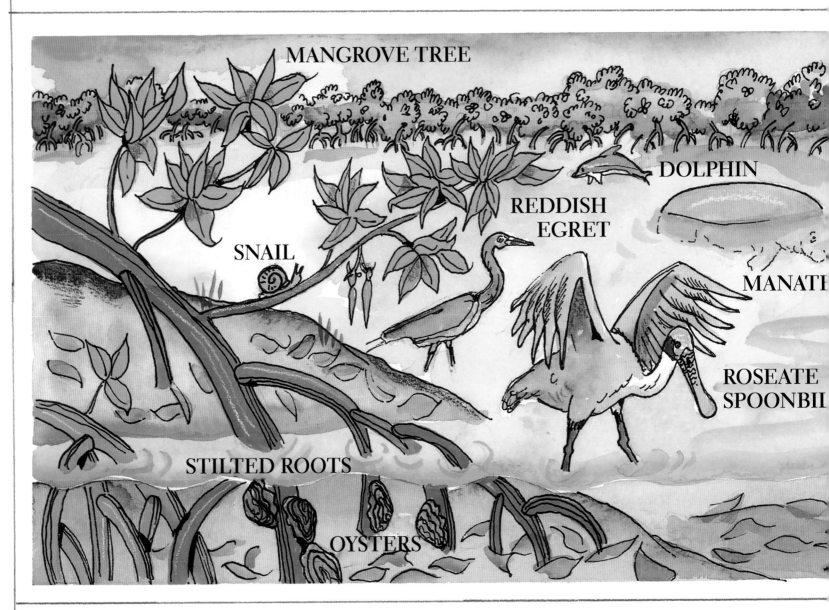

MANGROVE TREE

DOLPHIN

REDDISH
EGRET

SNAIL

MANATE

ROSEATE
SPOONBII

STILTED ROOTS

OYSTERS

Mangrove swamps thrive in a mixture of salt water and fresh water. They are found along tropical seacoasts. Mangrove swamps are named after the mangrove trees that grow there. These trees stand above the water on roots that look like stilts.

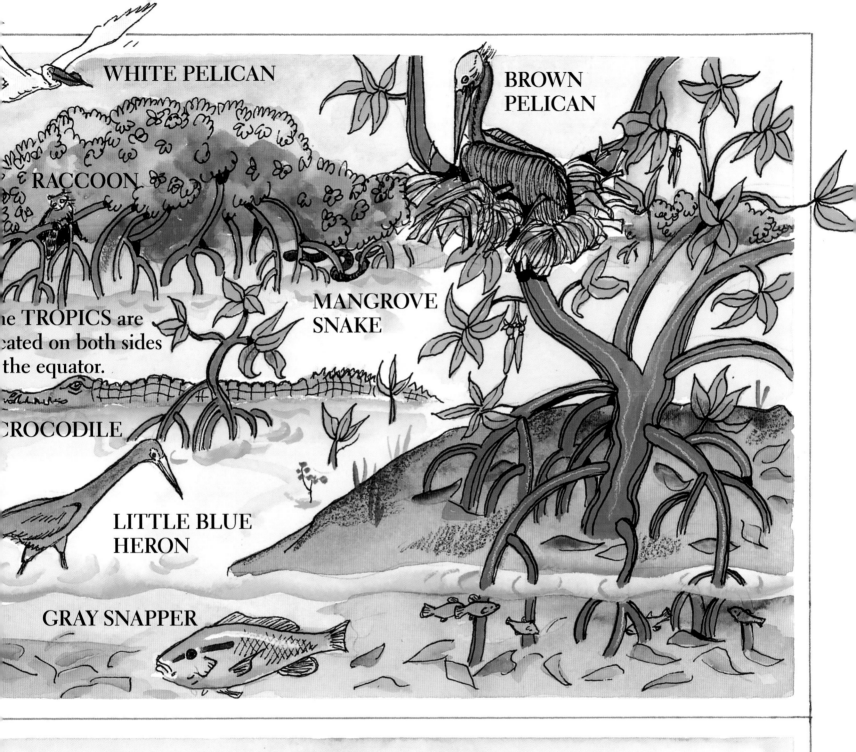

WHITE PELICAN

BROWN PELICAN

RACCOON

MANGROVE SNAKE

he TROPICS are
ated on both sides
the equator.

CROCODILE

LITTLE BLUE HERON

GRAY SNAPPER

These tangled roots are shelter for the many creatures that live there. Small fish swim around the roots, and barnacles and oysters grow on the roots under water. Brown pelicans and other waterbirds make their nests in its big branches.

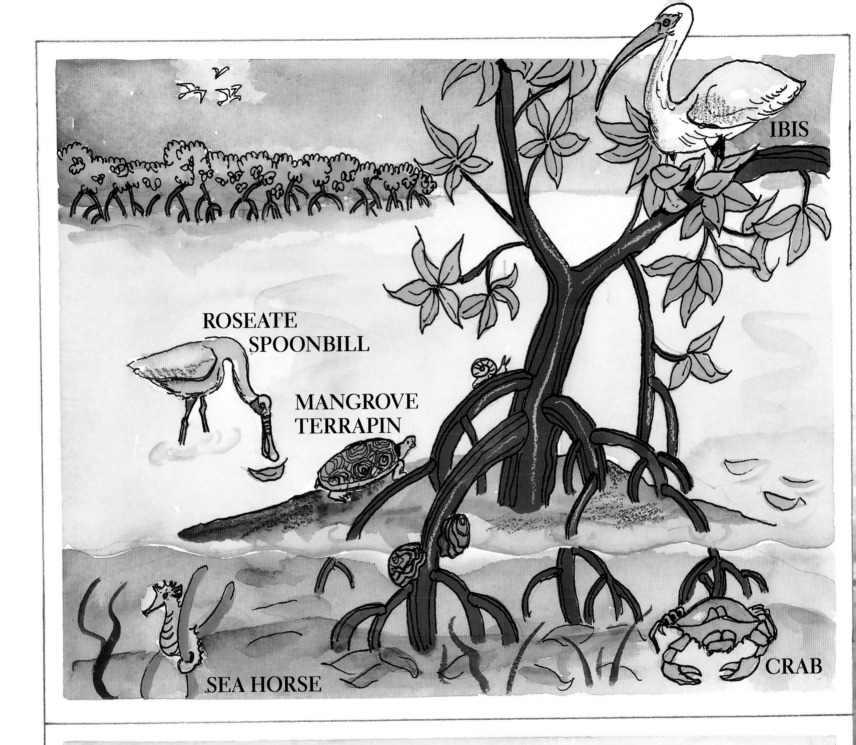

IBIS

ROSEATE
SPOONBILL

MANGROVE
TERRAPIN

SEA HORSE

CRAB

Mangrove trees allow land to form. When fallen leaves and branches and mud collect around a mangrove tree's roots, soil builds up. Bit by bit an island begins to take shape. It will become home for other plants and animals.

Each marsh and swamp is an ecosystem, which is a place
where plants and animals interact as a natural community.

EROSION is the wearing away of soil by wind and water.

Marshes and swamps are vital storage places for one of Earth's most precious resources—water. While storing large amounts of water, these areas reduce the chance of flooding in other places. Also, their plant life helps to stop the erosion of the surrounding land.

Many kinds of plants and animals need wetlands to survive. When wetlands are filled with dirt to create more land to build on, they are destroyed forever. Many acres of marshes and swamps have already been destroyed.

When marshes and swamps disappear, so do countless numbers of plants and animals. Many people are working to save our wetlands from destruction.

In some places boardwalks have been built over marshes and through swamps. That way people can walk into the natural beauty of swamps and marshes without disturbing the plants and animals that live there.

Marshes and swamps are wonderful places to explore. They have some of the most unusual landscapes in the world. They are home to many interesting creatures.

Many of these strange and beautiful places have been made refuges and preserves to protect their unusual plant and animal life. For the visitor they are always full of surprises.

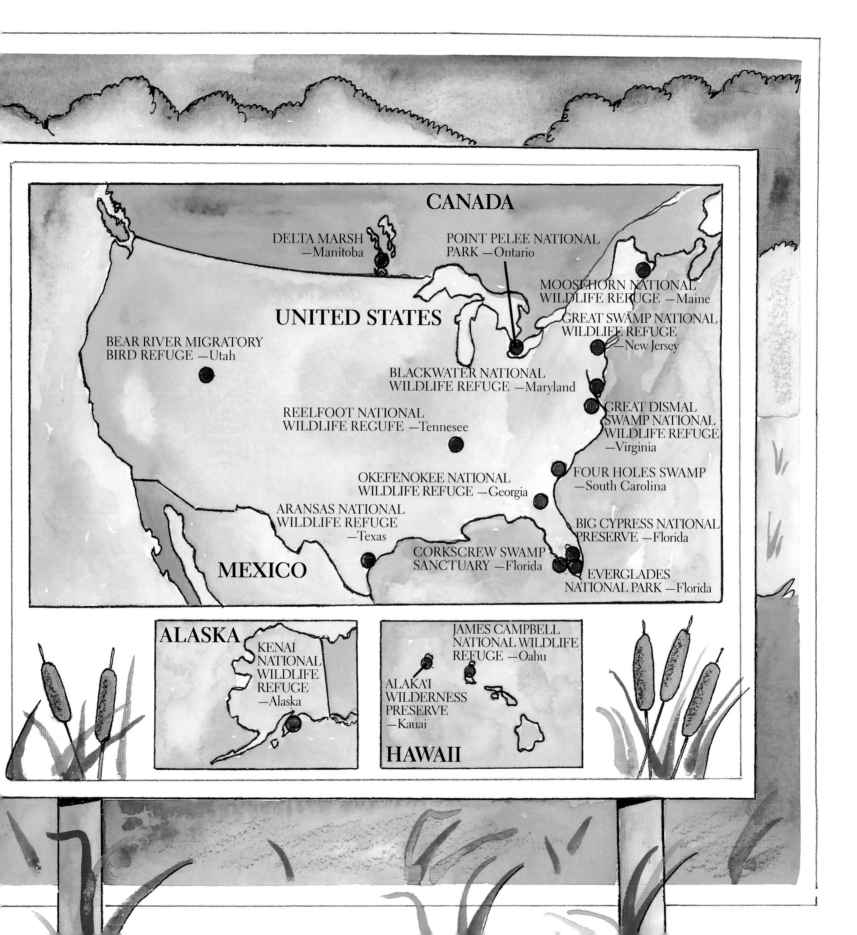

CANADA

UNITED STATES

MEXICO

DELTA MARSH
—Manitoba

POINT PELEE NATIONAL
PARK —Ontario

MOOSEHORN NATIONAL
WILDLIFE REFUGE —Maine

GREAT SWAMP NATIONAL
WILDLIFE REFUGE
—New Jersey

BEAR RIVER MIGRATORY
BIRD REFUGE —Utah

BLACKWATER NATIONAL
WILDLIFE REFUGE —Maryland

REELFOOT NATIONAL
WILDLIFE REGUFE —Tennesee

GREAT DISMAL
SWAMP NATIONAL
WILDLIFE REFUGE
—Virginia

OKEFENOKEE NATIONAL
WILDLIFE REFUGE —Georgia

FOUR HOLES SWAMP
—South Carolina

ARANSAS NATIONAL
WILDLIFE REFUGE
—Texas

BIG CYPRESS NATIONAL
PRESERVE —Florida

CORKSCREW SWAMP
SANCTUARY —Florida

EVERGLADES
NATIONAL PARK —Florida

ALASKA

KENAI
NATIONAL
WILDLIFE
REFUGE
—Alaska

JAMES CAMPBELL
NATIONAL WILDLIFE
REFUGE —Oahu

ALAKA'I
WILDERNESS
PRESERVE
—Kauai

HAWAII

MORE ABOUT WETLANDS

Fens are the rarest type of wetland and contain more plant and animal species than any other wetland. Fens are always fresh water because they are fed by groundwater.

About one half of all wetland areas in the United States are found in Alaska.

Wetlands are found on every continent except Antarctica.

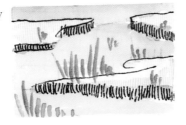

A bog is a wetland, too. Bogs are spongy, mossy wetlands where dead plants pile up faster than they can rot away. Walking on a bog feels like walking on a mattress. Each step seems to shake the whole bog.

Sections of some big cities were built where wetlands used to be. These include New Orleans, Miami, Boston, San Francisco, and Washington, D.C.

More than 170 countries are part of the Ramsar Convention, an international treaty devoted to preserving wetlands. The treaty has protected nearly half a million acres of wetland.

Marshes and swamps are important feeding places for migrating birds.

Less than half of the 215 million acres of wetlands that were in the continental United States still exist.